from SEA TO SHINING SEA

FLORIDA

By Dennis Brindell Fradin

CONSULTANTS

Charles R. McNeil, M.A., Historian, Museum of Florida History

Robert L. Hillerich, Ph.D., Consultant, Pinellas County Schools, Florida;
Visiting Professor, University of South Florida

CHILDRENS PRESS®

CHICAGO

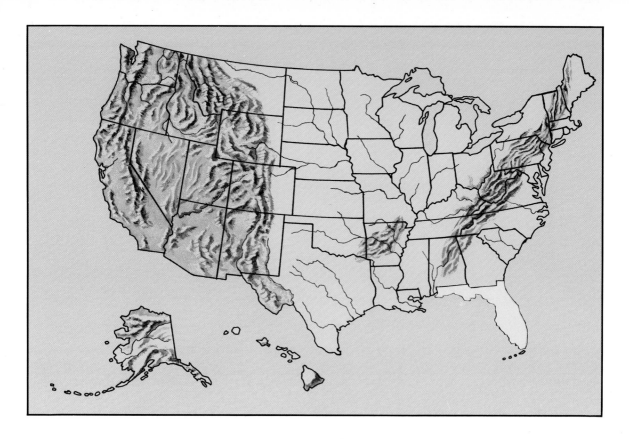

Florida is the southernmost of the fourteen states in the region called the South. The other southern states are Alabama, Arkansas, Delaware, Georgia, Kentucky, Louisiana, Maryland, Mississippi, North Carolina, South Carolina, Tennessee, Virginia, and West Virginia.

For my father, Myron Fradin, with love

For his help, the author thanks Michael Wisenbaker of the Division of Historical Resources, Florida Department of State

Front cover picture: a view of Miami Beach hotels across Indian Creek; page 1: a young man picking oranges in a Florida grove; back cover: Flamingo Harbor, Everglades National Park

Project Editor: Joan Downing
Design Director: Karen Kohn
Research Assistant: Judith Bloom Fradin
Typesetting: Graphic Connections, Inc.
Engraving: Liberty Photoengraving

FOURTH PRINTING, 1994.

Library of Congress Cataloging-in-Publication Data

Fradin, Dennis B.
   Florida / by Dennis Brindell Fradin.
   p.   cm. — (From sea to shining sea)
   Includes index.
   Summary: An introduction to the Sunshine State, its history, people, and sites of interest.
   ISBN 0-516-03809-5
   1. Florida—Juvenile literature. [1. Florida.] I. Title.
II. Series: Fradin, Dennis B. From sea to shining sea.
F311.3.F7 1992   91-32918
917.5904'63—dc20   CIP
                                                          AC

Table of Contents

Snorkelers in the Florida Keys

Introducing the Sunshine State 4

Palm Trees and Ocean Breezes 7

From Ancient Times Until Today 15

Floridians and Their Work 31

A Trip Through the Sunshine State 35

A Gallery of Famous Floridians 49

Did You Know? 54

Florida Information 56

Florida History 58

Map of Florida 60

Glossary 61

Index 63

Introducing the Sunshine State

Florida is a state in the southeastern corner of the United States. Florida is called the "Sunshine State." It has a warm climate and ocean beaches. They help make Florida one of the world's leading vacationlands. The state has many famous attractions. Two of them are Walt Disney World and the John F. Kennedy Space Center.

The Sunshine State is also a leader in farming. It is the number-one state for growing oranges and grapefruit. Florida is at or near the top of the list for growing sugarcane, bananas, strawberries, and tomatoes.

Several major historical events have occurred in Florida. St. Augustine was founded in Florida in 1565. It is the nation's oldest European town. About four hundred years later, in 1969, the first men to reach the moon blasted off from Florida. The Sunshine State has also been home to many famous people. They include American Indian leader Osceola, black leader James Weldon Johnson, and tennis star Chris Evert.

Overleaf: Cape Florida Lighthouse, Key Biscayne

A picture map of Florida

Florida has many other claims to fame. What state has alligators, sponges, and Portuguese men-of-war? Where did Marjorie Kinnan Rawlings and Ernest Hemingway do much of their writing? What state has a twenty-two-story capitol building? Where do the Dolphins and the Buccaneers play football? The answer to these questions is the Sunshine State: Florida.

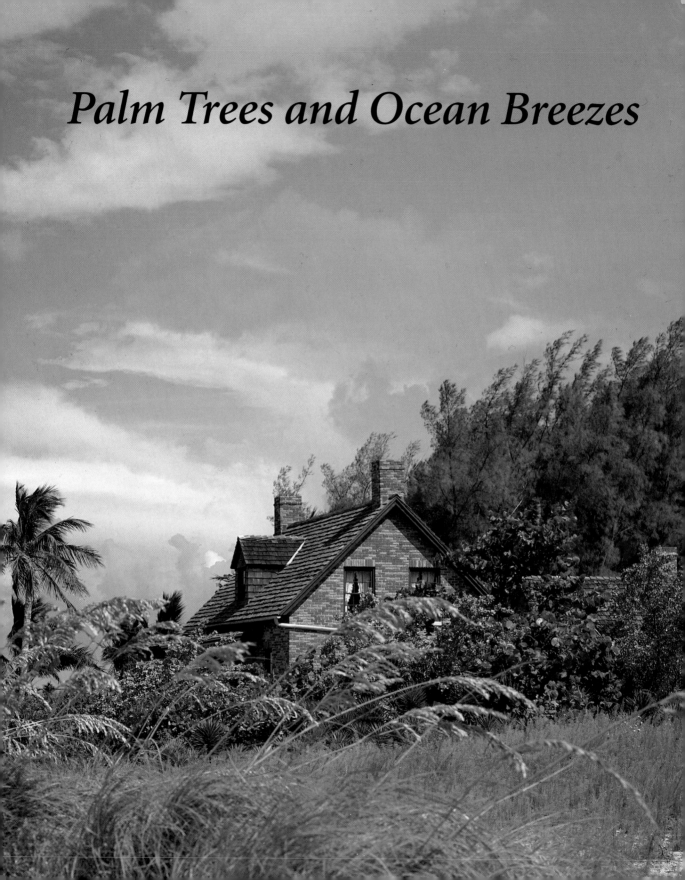

Palm Trees and Ocean Breezes

Palm Trees and Ocean Breezes

Florida is in the region of the country called the South. It is the southernmost of the fourteen southern states. Hawaii, in the Pacific Ocean, is the only state that is farther south than Florida.

Florida is a peninsula. A peninsula is land that is almost surrounded by water. The Atlantic Ocean is east of Florida. The Straits of Florida are to the south. The Gulf of Mexico lies to the west and to the south. Georgia and Alabama are to the north. A small part of Alabama is also to the west.

Below: Old Pass Lagoon, in Destin

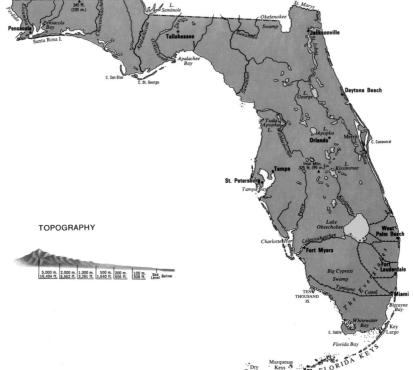

TOPOGRAPHY

| 5,000 m.
16,404 ft. | 2,000 m.
6,562 ft. | 1,000 m.
3,281 ft. | 500 m.
1,640 ft. | 200 m.
656 ft. | 100 m.
328 ft. | Sea
Level | Below |

There is plenty of water inside Florida, too. The state has nearly eight thousand lakes. The largest is Lake Okeechobee. It is the second-largest fresh-water lake totally within one state. The Suwannee is the most famous of Florida's rivers. The state song, "Swanee River," is about the Suwannee. (The song's composer, Stephen Foster, had his own spelling for the river). Other Florida rivers include the St. Johns, the St. Marys, the Apalachicola, and the Perdido. The Florida Everglades are the most famous of the state's swamplands. Grasses and trees grow in these water-covered lands.

Florida has no mountains. Most of the state is made up of low flatlands. That region is called the Coastal Plains. The hilly Florida Uplands region takes up the rest of the state. Florida's highest point is only 345 feet above sea level. It is in the uplands

Cypress Gardens (above) is near Winter Haven.

The Salt River (above) is shown at the town of Crystal River, on the Gulf of Mexico.

Hibiscus flowers at Fairchild Tropical Garden (above) and orchids at Parrot Jungle (below left) are among the many varieties of flowers that grow in Florida. Coconuts grow on coconut palm trees (below right).

of the northwestern panhandle. No other state's highest point is that low.

Many islands off the coast are also part of Florida. The Florida Keys are famous islands to the south. The Ten Thousand Islands along the Gulf Coast are another well-known island group.

PLANTS AND ANIMALS

Florida is a Spanish word meaning "full of flowers." The name fits. Orchids, lilies, and many other wildflowers help make Florida beautiful. Many kinds of trees not seen in the North also grow there. Florida's palms include sabal palms (the state tree) and coconut palms. Mangrove trees grow in shallow ocean waters. Other trees found in Florida include

magnolias, oaks, and pines. Some trees seem to have beards hanging from them. This is Spanish moss. It is a plant that grows on trees in the South.

Florida has a wide variety of ocean life. Whales, dolphins, sea horses, starfish, and huge loggerhead sea turtles can be seen along the coast. The dolphins often swim near people. They like to show off their water tricks. Manatees also live in Florida's coastal waters. Unfortunately, people have killed off most of the world's manatees. There are about one thousand manatees in Florida waters. That may be the largest manatee colony remaining.

Florida has a river and a county named Manatee.

Lobsters, shrimp, crabs, and oysters are among the shellfish found along the coast. Florida's ocean fish include tarpon, pompano, red snapper, and sailfish.

Florida ocean life includes manatees (left) and bluestripe grunts (right).

Fish-eating birds called anhingas (above) are common in Florida's swamps.

The Florida panther is the state animal.

It is best to avoid some of Florida's water creatures. Florida's swamps and rivers are home to many alligators. Sharks sometimes approach the seashore. Swimmers should also stay away from Portuguese men-of-war. They are floating animals that look like big balloons. They give a painful sting.

Deer can be seen in Florida's forests. The Key deer is native to the Florida Keys. This small deer has become very rare. The same is true of the Florida panther. This panther is a large cat that looks like a mountain lion. Other Florida animals include bears, bobcats, foxes, beavers, otters, and skunks.

Florida is a bird-watcher's heaven. Pelicans live along the coast. They dive into the water and catch fish in their pouches. Storks, mockingbirds (the state bird), woodpeckers, cranes, herons, bald eagles, egrets, and water turkeys are also found in the state.

CLIMATE

Because Florida is so far south, its climate is warm. January temperatures sometimes top 70 degrees Fahrenheit. Summer temperatures often top 90 degrees Fahrenheit. Ocean waters help keep Florida from being even hotter in the summer. The waters act as a kind of giant air conditioner.

The ocean produces one dangerous kind of weather, though. Huge sea storms called hurricanes sometimes strike Florida. A big hurricane slammed into southern Florida in 1935. That storm killed more than four hundred people. The United States has developed a fine hurricane warning system since then. It has lowered the number of deaths from these terrible storms.

This wading bird called a roseate spoonbill feeds on marine life in Everglades National Park.

*From Ancient Times
Until Today*

FROM ANCIENT TIMES UNTIL TODAY

About two million years ago, the Ice Age began. Huge sheets of ice covered much of what is now the northern United States. The ice didn't reach Florida. Many animals in the North did what people do today. They went south to Florida to escape the cold! During the Ice Age, Florida had a great variety of animals. There were mastodons. These huge animals looked like large, hairy elephants. There were saber-toothed tigers with teeth 8 inches long. Florida was also home to camels, horses, wolves, and even lions.

At times, Florida was covered by inland oceans. The region was among the last parts of North America to emerge from the sea. The last ocean left Florida only about 120,000 years ago.

THE NATIVE AMERICANS

People first reached Florida at least twelve thousand years ago. These first Floridians were prehistoric Indians. They hunted deer and other animals. They also gathered berries and other plant foods.

Five main groups of American Indians (Native

Opposite: A space shuttle launch, Cape Canaveral

In the 1500s, many American Indian groups surrounded their villages with tall wooden fences called palisades.

Early Florida Indians dried and smoked game for use during the winter.

Americans) lived in Florida by the 1500s. They were the Ais, the Apalachees, the Calusas, the Tequestas, and the Timucuas. Some Indians grew corn, beans, and squash. Those who lived in the woodlands hunted. Coastal Indians fished and gathered shellfish.

SPAIN CLAIMS FLORIDA

In 1492, Christopher Columbus made a famous voyage. He sailed to the New World for Spain. Columbus explored Cuba and other Caribbean islands. He thought he was near India. That is why the Caribbean islands were named the West Indies. Spanish people soon moved to the West Indies.

Those Spaniards decided to explore the mainland of what is now the United States. In 1513, Spanish explorer Juan Ponce de León sailed north from Puerto Rico. He hoped to find gold.

Ponce de León landed near the present-day city of St. Augustine, Florida. He was the first known European in Florida. He also named the region. Perhaps he chose the name *Florida* because of the wildflowers he saw there. Or perhaps he did so because it was Easter time. The Spanish called Easter *Pascua Florida*. Ponce de León did not find gold in Florida. But he did claim Florida for Spain. Other Spaniards reached the Florida coast over the next few years.

Ponce de León returned to Florida in 1521. This time, he brought settlers. Soon after they landed, the Spaniards were attacked by Indians. Ponce de León was struck by an Indian arrow. The Spaniards fled Florida with their wounded leader.

The Spaniards made more attempts to settle Florida over the next forty years. In 1559, they began a settlement near what is now Pensacola. But a hurricane helped end this colony.

In 1564, French people built Fort Caroline near what is now Jacksonville. This action worried the Spaniards. Spain was finally ready to take control of Florida.

The king of Spain sent Don Pedro Menéndez de Avilés to Florida in 1565. Four hundred soldiers went with Menéndez. They captured Fort Caroline. They also founded a settlement nearby. They called it St. Augustine. It was the first permanent European town in what is now the United States.

Spain held Florida rather weakly for about two hundred years. Spanish soldiers built forts in Florida. Spanish priests built missions. There, they taught the Indians about Christianity. Few Spanish families moved to Florida, however.

In 1565, Spanish soldiers captured Fort Caroline (above) from the French. Then they founded the town of St. Augustine (below).

Twenty Years of English Rule

England was the main country to settle what is now the United States. England began its first American colony—Virginia—in 1607. By 1773, England ruled thirteen American colonies.

England tried to take Florida away from Spain. English troops from Georgia tried to seize Florida several times between 1740 and 1742. The English finally took control of Florida in 1763.

England split Florida in two. Most of what is now Florida became East Florida. The region west of the Apalachicola River was made part of West Florida. England's hold on Florida was never very strong, though. Few English people moved there during the twenty years of English rule.

Parts of present-day Alabama, Mississippi, and Louisiana were also in West Florida.

Starting in 1765, the thirteen American colonies north of Florida began to rebel against England. This revolt grew into the Revolutionary War (1775-1783). Americans fought it to break free of England and create the United States.

Florida stayed loyal to England during the war. It was England's only territory in what is now the United States to do so.

Spain saw the Revolutionary War as a chance to hurt England. Spain sided with the Americans dur-

Andrew Jackson (above, on the left) at Pensacola during the First Seminole War.

ing the war. The Spaniards captured West Florida from England in 1781. In 1783, the United States won the Revolutionary War. As part of the peace treaty, Spain regained all of Florida that year.

THE SECOND SPANISH PERIOD

Spain ruled Florida for another thirty-eight years. But during that time, Americans started to move to Florida. They demanded that Florida become part of the United States.

In November 1814, American general Andrew Jackson and his troops captured Pensacola from the Spaniards. In 1817, the Seminole Indians began attacking American settlers in Florida. The Seminoles were Creek Indians who came to Florida from Georgia and Alabama in the early 1700s. They became angry as Americans took their land. During the First Seminole War (1817-1818), Jackson defeated the Seminoles.

Spain saw that the Americans wouldn't rest until they had Florida. Spain made a deal with the United States. It took effect in 1821. The United States cancelled a $5 million debt owed by Spain. In return, Florida became part of the United States.

FLORIDA BECOMES THE TWENTY-SEVENTH STATE

At first, Florida was not a state. It was a territory. It was land owned by the United States. Andrew Jackson became Florida's military governor.

The Americans and the Seminoles continued to fight over the best farmland. The United States government tried to make the Seminoles move to Oklahoma. Most Seminoles chose to fight rather than leave. Under their leader, Osceola, the Seminoles fought the Second Seminole War (1835-1842). About fifteen hundred American troops and a large number of Seminoles died during the war. Most of the surviving Seminoles were forced to move to Oklahoma. Some Seminoles stayed in Florida. They hid in the swamps. The defeat of the

The Seminoles, under their leader Osceola, attacked Fort King (below) during the Second Seminole War.

21

Indians opened more land to settlement. By 1845, about 66,500 settlers lived in Florida. Florida became the twenty-seventh state on March 3, 1845. Tallahassee became the state capital, and it still is.

The Civil War

In Florida and the other southern states, black slaves grew the crops on their owners' plantations. By 1850, nearly half of the ninety thousand Floridians were black slaves. In the North, slavery had been outlawed. Northerners began pressing the South to end slavery.

Abraham Lincoln was elected president of the United States in 1860. White southerners feared that Lincoln would end slavery. One by one, the southern states seceded from (left) the United States. Florida left on January 10, 1861. Florida and ten other southern states joined together as the Confederate States of America—known for short as the Confederacy.

The Civil War began on April 12, 1861. It was fought between the Confederacy (the South) and the Union (the North). About fifteen thousand Floridians served in the Confederate army. On February 20, 1864, the Confederates won the

Before the Civil War, these black slaves picked cotton on their owner's plantation.

Florida was the third southern state to secede, following South Carolina and Mississippi.

state's biggest Civil War battle. It was called the Battle of Olustee. About a year later, northern troops marched toward Tallahassee. They hoped to capture the Florida capital. But the Confederates prevented this by winning the Battle of Natural Bridge on March 6, 1865. Some Tallahassee schoolboys took part in this Confederate victory.

The Tallahassee schoolboys who took part in the Battle of Natural Bridge were known as the "Baby Corps."

The Confederates did well in Florida, but the North won the war on April 9, 1865. Florida and the other southern states had to free their slaves. Florida rejoined the Union on June 25, 1868.

YEARS OF GROWTH

The late 1800s were years of great growth for Florida. Swamps were drained. Families moved to

A Confederate battery at Pensacola during the Civil War

Passengers got off this Atlantic Coast Line train about 1900 to pick fruit in Bartow.

Julia Tuttle (below) helped bring the railroad to Biscayne Bay.

Florida. They grew oranges and grapefruit. Railroads were built. They linked Florida to the rest of the country. Railroad builder Henry Plant helped develop the city of Tampa in the 1880s and 1890s. Rare cold weather led to the development of the Miami area.

The winter of 1894-95 was unusually cold in Florida. Much of the orange crop in the middle of the state was ruined. Julia S. Tuttle was one of the pioneers along Biscayne Bay. The oranges where she lived had survived. To prove it, Tuttle sent some orange blossoms to Henry Flagler. He was another railroad builder. Tuttle made Flagler an offer. She wanted him to extend his railroad to Biscayne Bay. If he did that, she would give him land for a city.

It was an offer Flagler couldn't refuse. His railroad reached Biscayne Bay in 1896. That year, the city of Miami was founded on the bay.

In the early 1900s, more people flocked to Florida. Many went there to live. Even more went there to vacation. New hotels and even towns were built. Miami Beach was begun in 1912. Fort Lauderdale, Hialeah, Hollywood, and Coral Gables were also begun in the early 1900s.

During World War I (1914-1918), more people visited Florida. Travel to Europe was no longer safe. In 1917, the United States entered the war. Military training camps were built at Pensacola, Jacksonville, and Miami. About forty-two thousand Floridians helped the United States and its allies win the war.

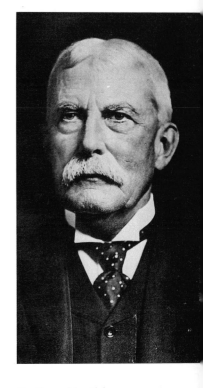

Railroad builder
Henry M. Flagler

HARD TIMES

Florida suffered some hard times in the 1920s and 1930s. A hurricane slammed into Miami in 1926. Hundreds of people were killed. Thousands were injured. Another hurricane struck Florida in 1928. This time, eighteen hundred people around Lake Okeechobee died. People who read about the hurricanes were afraid to come to Florida. This hurt the tourism business.

A depression is a period of hardship when many people lose their jobs and money.

To make things worse, a depression hit Florida in 1926. This was three years before the Great Depression (1929-1939) struck the whole nation. More than two hundred Florida banks closed during those thirteen years of hardship. Thousands of Floridians were left penniless. Hotels and restaurants closed. People could no longer afford to visit Florida.

The biggest war in history helped end the Great Depression. This was World War II (1939-1945). The United States entered the war in 1941. Many more military bases were built in Florida during the war. More than 250,000 Florida men and women helped the United States and its allies win the war.

Troops exercising at Miami Beach during World War II

A NEW GROWTH SPURT AND PROBLEMS

In the 1950s, Florida helped give birth to the space age. The United States began launching spacecraft from Florida's Cape Canaveral in 1958. *Explorer I*, the nation's first space satellite, was launched from Cape Canaveral that year. On July 16, 1969, *Apollo 11* blasted off from Cape Canaveral. Four days later, it landed the first men on the moon.

Florida began to attract more people than ever before. Many people had avoided Florida because of its hot summers. Air conditioning came into widespread use during the 1950s. It helped create a population explosion. Between 1950 and 1990, Florida's population rose from 2.8 million to almost 13 million.

These members of the military took part in the Victory Day Parade in Tallahassee after World War II.

Many of the newcomers were retired people. Thousands more came from Cuba and Haiti. Cuba had a change in government in 1959. About three hundred thousand Cubans moved to the Miami area in the 1960s. They didn't want to live under the new Cuban government. During the 1980s, more than one hundred thousand people from Cuba and Haiti moved to Florida. The Haitians were fleeing poverty and a harsh government.

Walt Disney World opened near Orlando in 1971. This famous amusement park has drawn many millions of visitors to the state.

Yet, all was not well in Florida. Even in the 1950s, black Floridians were still being mistreated.

EPCOT Center (below) is part of the Walt Disney World complex near Orlando.

Many were kept from voting. Black children were not allowed to attend the same schools as white children. Blacks were kept off certain beaches and out of some hotels and restaurants. This was true throughout much of the country.

Congress passed laws to end this injustice during the 1960s. The laws helped. By the 1970s, thousands of black Floridians were voting for the first time. Black children and white children went to school together in many Florida cities. People of all colors shared public places. But many black Floridians still feel that they can't get good jobs and housing.

Illegal drugs are another huge problem in Florida. Every state has drug addicts. But Florida has a special problem. Tons of drugs enter the United States through the Miami area each year. Law officers have tried to stop this drug trade. But it is a hard problem to solve.

Florida's growing population also presents problems. The state has had trouble providing services for all its people. Florida needs more and better schools. It needs to improve its health care. Ways must be found to solve Florida's water- and air-pollution problems. These are some of the challenges Floridians face in the 1990s and beyond.

The people shown above escaped from Cuba and came to Key West in an open boat in 1961.

Black voters joined white voters (below) during voter registration at Tallahassee City Hall in the 1960s.

Floridians and Their Work

FLORIDIANS AND THEIR WORK

As of 1990, almost 13 million people were living in Florida. The only states with more people were California, New York, and Texas. About one-fifth of all Floridians are over sixty-five years old. No other state has as large a percentage of senior citizens. Florida is also home to 1.8 million blacks, 1.6 million Hispanics, and 150,000 Asians. Only a handful of states have more people in these three groups. About fifteen hundred Seminoles live in the state.

The people who live in Florida come from many different backgrounds.

Forty million people visit Florida each year. They make tourism a giant business in Florida. Large numbers of Floridians work in hotels and motels and at other tourist-related jobs.

Counting the tourists, there are more than 50 million people in Florida each year. Those people need such items as food and clothing. More than a million Floridians work in stores where they sell a wide range of goods.

Florida is also a manufacturing leader. About half a million Floridians work in factories. They package such foods as orange juice, vegetables, and fish. They make computers, telephones, furniture,

paper, fertilizer, cigars, chemicals, robots, missiles, airplanes, and spacecraft.

Florida is a leader in farming. It is the leading state for growing oranges. Each year, Florida produces 15 billion pounds of oranges. This comes to about 40 billion oranges, or eight for each person on earth. Florida also leads the nation in growing grapefruit, tangerines, limes, sugarcane, and watermelons. The state is a leader in growing tomatoes, sweet corn, avocados, green peppers, bananas, and strawberries. And it is a major producer of beef cattle, milk, and chickens.

Florida has an Orange County and towns named Orange City, Orange Park, and Port Orange.

Tourism (left) and the aircraft industry (right) are among Florida's important industries.

Florida is also a leader in fishing. Shrimp, lobsters, crabs, and oysters are major Florida shellfish. If you use a real sponge in your home, it may have come from Florida. Tarpon Springs, on the Gulf of Mexico, is a famous sponge-fishing center.

Nearly a million Floridians work for the government. The state's many military bases and public parklands help account for this. Each week, Florida's population grows by about six thousand people. The new Floridians need housing. More than a third of a million Floridians work in construction.

Shellfish (left) and fruit (right) are important Florida products.

Overleaf: Cinderella Castle at Walt Disney World

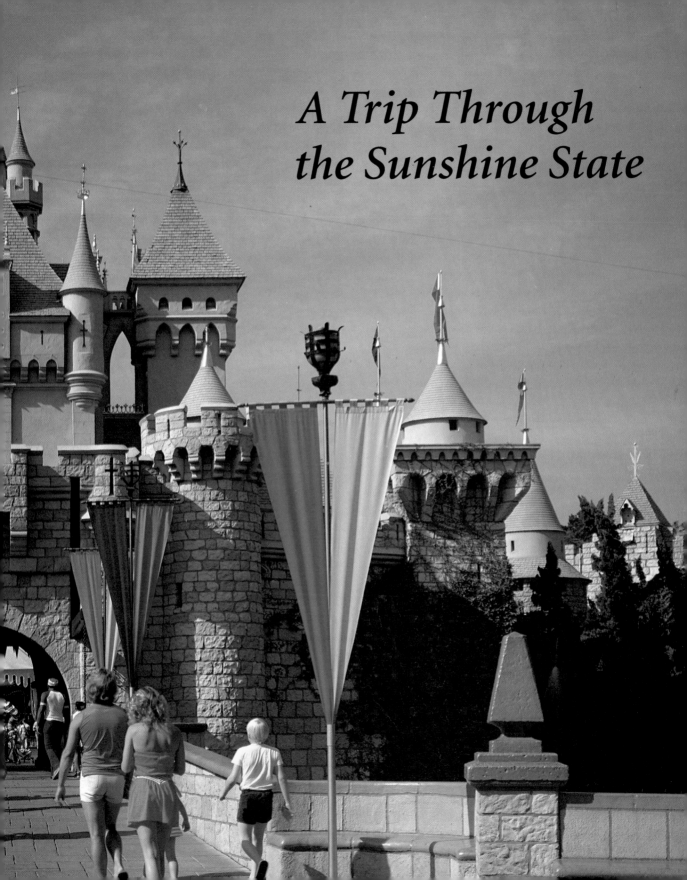

A Trip Through the Sunshine State

A Trip Through the Sunshine State

F lorida is famous for its lovely beaches and warm weather. It is also famous as the launching site for United States spacecraft. The state is home to Walt Disney World, EPCOT Center, and many interesting cities and historic sites.

Jacksonville

A father and his daughter (below) enjoy a Marco Island beach.

A plantation is a large southern farm that used slave labor until 1865.

Jacksonville would be a good place to begin a trip through Florida. The city lies on the St. Johns River in northeastern Florida. Jacksonville was begun in 1822. Jacksonville's 850 square miles make it the nation's second-biggest city in area. Only Juneau, Alaska, is larger. Its 635,230 people also make it Florida's largest city in population. Paper, foods, cigars, and chemicals are made in Jacksonville. The city is a center for banking and insurance.

Fort Caroline National Memorial is a Jacksonville-area landmark. It has been built to look like the French fort of 1564. Kingsley Plantation is near the fort. Built in 1813, it is the state's oldest plantation house.

Jacksonville has two fine-arts museums. In 1961, Ninah Cummer's collection became the seed of the Cummer Gallery of Art. Modern paintings and ancient Indian artworks are displayed at the Jacksonville Art Museum. Jacksonville also hosts the Gator Bowl college football game.

The fort called Castillo de San Marcos (left) is in St. Augustine (right).

FLORIDA'S EAST COAST

One of America's most historic towns is south of Jacksonville. St. Augustine is the oldest European-built town in the nation. Castillo de San Marcos at St. Augustine is America's oldest stone fort.

Spaniards built it in the 1600s. They used *coquina*, a rock made of shells and coral. St. Augustine's oldest known house dates from the early 1700s. It is the Gonzalez-Alvarez House.

The world's oldest oceanarium is south of St. Augustine. It is called Marineland of Florida. Hundreds of sea animals can be seen there.

Many Florida cities have the word *beach* in their names because they lie along the ocean. Fernandina Beach, Ormond Beach, Vero Beach, and West Palm Beach all lie along Florida's east coast. Daytona Beach is south of Marineland. It is the home of a

An oceanarium houses ocean animals for public viewing

Below: A view of West Palm Beach

famous auto racetrack. It is called the Daytona International Speedway.

The Mary McLeod Bethune house is also in Daytona Beach. Bethune (1875-1955) was a great black educator. In 1904, she opened a school in Daytona Beach. It became Bethune-Cookman College. The college is a famous school for training black teachers.

Daytona International Speedway

The Kennedy Space Center

John F. Kennedy Space Center is at Cape Canaveral. Many important space flights have blasted off from there. Visitors can see rockets and other items relating to space travel.

Florida's coastal birds are interesting. Pelican Island National Wildlife Refuge is south of the space center. President Theodore Roosevelt founded the refuge in 1903. It is the oldest national wildlife refuge in the country. The pelicans and other birds at the refuge let people get very close to them.

Several major cities lie along the Atlantic Ocean in southeastern Florida. Fort Lauderdale is the state's seventh-largest city. A teacher, Ivy Cromartie Stranahan, helped found Fort Lauderdale in the early 1900s. The International Swimming Hall of Fame in Fort Lauderdale honors great swimmers. Butterfly World is near Fort Lauderdale. Visitors can walk through its gardens among the butterflies.

Miami (above) celebrates its one hundredth birthday in 1996.

Parrots perch on the arm of a tourist at Parrot Jungle (below).

Miami is near the southern tip of Florida. With 358,548 people, Miami is Florida's second-largest city. More than half of Miami's people are foreign-born. Most of them are from Cuba. Spanish is the main language in parts of Miami.

Miami is a leading city for making clothing. Furniture is also made there. But tourism is the region's biggest business. Many of the tourists come to Miami Beach, a seaside city near Miami.

Parrot Jungle is one of the Miami area's most interesting attractions. It has hundreds of parrots, flamingos, and other birds. Monkey Jungle is home to more than five hundred monkeys. Miami is also a sports center. On New Year's Day, the city hosts the

Orange Bowl college football game. The Miami Dolphins are the city's pro football team. The Miami Heat are its pro basketball team.

THE FLORIDA KEYS

The Florida Keys lie off the southern Florida coast. The name key comes from *cayo*, Spanish for "small island." English-speaking people changed cayo to key. There are hundreds of Florida Keys. About thirty of the main islands can be reached by car on the Overseas Highway.

The Overseas Highway (below) connects many of the islands in the Florida Keys.

Coral reefs are ocean ridges created over thousands of years by tiny animals called coral.

Treasure hunter Mel Fisher (below) shows off some of the gold from the Spanish treasure ship Atocha.

Key Largo is the first of the keys along the Overseas Highway. John Pennekamp Coral Reef State Park is near Key Largo. It is one of the world's few underwater parks. Some people dive into the water to look at the coral reefs. Others view the coral through glass-bottomed boats.

Key West is the last stop on the Overseas Highway. This island has been home to some famous authors. Ernest Hemingway's home is open to visitors. Hemingway wrote his novel *For Whom the Bell Tolls* while living there.

The Florida Keys attract many underwater treasure hunters. They look for Spanish treasure ships and other sunken vessels. Treasure hunter Mel Fisher made a great discovery off Key West in 1985. Fisher found the *Atocha*, a Spanish treasure ship that went down in a hurricane in 1622. Silver, emeralds, gold, and other treasure from the *Atocha* are worth about $400 million. The Mel Fisher Maritime Heritage Society Museum in Key West displays many treasures from the *Atocha*.

FLORIDA'S WEST COAST

Florida's west coast is called its Gulf Coast. It lies along the arm of the Atlantic Ocean called the Gulf

of Mexico. Fort Myers, Naples, and Clearwater are popular vacation spots along the Gulf Coast. Sanibel and Captiva islands are among North America's best places to collect seashells.

Sarasota is north of Captiva Island. The famous Ringling Brothers and Barnum & Bailey Circus spent the winter in Sarasota for many years. The Ringling Museum of Art is in Sarasota.

Florida's fourth-biggest city is St. Petersburg. The city is north of Sarasota on Tampa Bay. "St. Pete" calls itself the country's "Winter Baseball Capital." Several major-league teams hold spring training in the area. In 1991, eighteen big-league teams trained in Florida. They make up what is called the "Grapefruit League."

Collecting shells on Sanibel Island (left) and visiting the Ringling Museum of Art in Sarasota (right) are two activities enjoyed by visitors to Florida.

The children above are enjoying Busch Gardens.

The Blue Angels flight squadron (below) is based at the Pensacola Naval Air Station.

Tampa, the state's third-largest city, is across Tampa Bay from St. Pete. The two cities are so close together that they are often called Tampa-St. Pete.

Long ago, pirates sailed in the waters around present-day Tampa. The people of Tampa have fun with their pirate history. The city's pro-football team is called the Buccaneers. Each February, Tampa holds the Gasparilla Pirate Invasion. A ship filled with "pirates" pretends to attack the city. The festival was named for Gasparilla, a pirate who reportedly robbed ships off Florida.

A famous park with an African theme is in Tampa. It is called Busch Gardens. African animals and plants can be seen in the park. There are also exciting rides.

Pensacola lies along the Gulf of Mexico in the Florida panhandle. The Pensacola Naval Air Station is near Pensacola. A flight squadron known for its thrilling air shows is based there. The squadron is called the Blue Angels.

THE FLORIDA INTERIOR

The inner part of Florida has fields of crops and orchards with orange and grapefruit trees. In places, cowboys can be seen tending cattle. The interior also has some important cities.

Tallahassee, the state capital, is in northern Florida. In the 1500s, the Apalachee Indians had a town where the city now stands. They called it Tallahassee, meaning "old town." The Spanish settlement that grew up here in the 1600s kept the Indian name.

Florida has one of the nation's newest capitol buildings. It is a twenty-two-story skyscraper that opened in 1977. The Museum of Florida History is also in Tallahassee. Mastodon bones and treasures from a sunken Spanish ship are among its highlights.

Florida has many springs. These are places from which water comes out of cracks in the ground.

Florida's new state capitol building stands behind the old one in this picture. Tallahassee has been the state capital since 1823.

45

Sea World (above) is near Orlando.

Wakulla Springs, outside Tallahassee, is 185 feet deep. It is one of the country's deepest springs.

Gainesville is southeast of Tallahassee. It is the home of the University of Florida. Founded in 1853, it is the oldest school of higher learning in the state.

Orlando is southeast of Gainesville. Walt Disney World is near Orlando. This huge amusement park offers rides and a movie studio. EPCOT Center is also part of Disney World. It shows what life in the future may be like. Sea World, near Orlando, exhibits sharks, dolphins, whales, and manatees.

The Everglades, in southern Florida, would be a good place to end a Florida trip. This huge swampy area takes up 2,750 square miles.

Everglades National Park occupies part of the Everglades. Few people live in the park. There are plenty of animals, though. Alligators, crocodiles, and deer can be seen. Turtles weighing hundreds of pounds can be spotted, as can many kinds of water birds. A few Florida panthers also live in the Everglades. Unfortunately, people have badly polluted the Everglades. Many people are working to clean up these famous swamplands.

People hiking in the Everglades (left) may be lucky enough to see a green sea turtle (right).

A
Gallery
of Famous
Floridians

A GALLERY OF FAMOUS FLORIDIANS

Many famous people have lived in Florida. They include Native American leaders, inventors, authors, lawmakers, musicians, civil-rights leaders, and athletes.

Opposite: Creek-Seminole leader Osceola

Osceola (1804?-1838) was born a Creek Indian in Alabama. After his people lost the Creek War of 1813-14, Osceola went to Florida. In Florida, the Creeks were called Seminoles. Osceola led the Seminoles in their fight to stay in Florida. He and his warriors defeated U.S. troops during the 1830s. U.S. soldiers finally pretended that they wanted to talk to Osceola. When Osceola reached the meeting, the soldiers captured him. He was imprisoned in South Carolina, where he died at about the age of thirty-four.

John Gorrie (1803-1855) was born in South Carolina. He became a doctor and moved to Apalachicola, Florida. Gorrie felt that Florida's heat was harmful to sick people. During the 1840s, he built an ice-making machine to cool the rooms of patients. It helped result in the invention of air conditioning. Gorrie also served as the mayor of Apalachicola.

Henry Morrison Flagler (1830-1913) was born in New York State. He helped John D. Rockefeller form the Standard Oil Company. Flagler poured much of his fortune into Florida. He built a railroad. He also built a number of hotels, schools, and hospitals. Flagler County and Flagler Beach in northeastern Florida were named for him.

James Weldon Johnson (1871-1938) was born in Jacksonville. He was a man of many talents. In 1897, he became one of the first black lawyers to be licensed in Florida. He worked as a school principal in Jacksonville. He was a poet, a statesman, and a civil-rights leader. James Weldon Johnson also wrote songs. One of them, "Lift Every Voice and Sing," is known as the black national anthem.

The great black leader **A. Philip Randolph** (1889-1979) was born in Crescent City. Randolph was a labor leader. He helped organize black workers into unions. These are groups that fight for the

Black leader A. Philip Randolph (left) and author Marjorie Kinnan Rawlings (right)

rights of working people. In 1963, at the age of seventy-four, Randolph helped organize the most famous civil-rights march in U.S. history. More than two hundred thousand people came to this "March on Washington." Dr. Martin Luther King, Jr., made his "I Have a Dream" speech at this march.

Claude Pepper (1900-1989) was born in Alabama. At the age of twenty-five, he moved to Florida. He became a famous lawmaker. Pepper represented Florida in the U.S. Senate and then the House of Representatives for more than forty years. He helped pass the country's first minimum-wage law. It made sure that workers received decent pay. He did other work to help poor and black Americans. But Pepper was best known as the champion of the elderly. He played a big role in raising the retirement age for millions of workers. People no longer were forced to retire at age sixty-five. Pepper was the oldest member of the U.S. Congress when he died at the age of eighty-eight.

U. S. Congressman Claude Pepper

Marjorie Kinnan Rawlings (1896-1953) was born in Washington, D.C. She sold her first story when she was eleven years old. For a time, she worked as a newspaper writer. In 1928, Rawlings moved to Florida. There she wrote many fine stories. Her novel *The Yearling* won a Pulitzer Prize in 1939.

Author Marjory Stoneman Douglas

Motion-picture actor Sidney Poitier

Author **Marjory Stoneman Douglas** was born in Minnesota in 1890. She moved to Florida in 1915 and began writing about the state. Her works include *The Everglades: River of Grass, Alligator Crossing,* and *Hurricane.* Douglas was also a leader in the effort to create Everglades National Park. As of 1991, she was 101 years old and still living in Florida.

Julian "Cannonball" Adderley (1928-1975) was born in Tampa. Adderley formed his own jazz band as a high-school student in Tallahassee. He later became a great jazz saxophonist. Another famous entertainer, actor **Sidney Poitier**, was born in Miami in 1927. Poitier won the 1963 Academy Award for his role in *Lilies of the Field.* His other films include *Guess Who's Coming to Dinner* and *In the Heat of the Night.*

Baseball pitchers **Steve Carlton** and **Dwight Gooden** both came from Florida. Carlton was born in Miami in 1944. In twenty-four major-league seasons, he won 329 games and was named the National League's best pitcher four times. Gooden was born in Tampa in 1964. He was the 1984 National League Rookie of the Year. Gooden has had a great career since then. Basketball star **Artis Gilmore** was born in Chipley in 1945. Gilmore's

Baseball pitcher Dwight Gooden (left) and tennis star Chris Evert (right)

shooting percentage of .599 (about six in every ten shots) is the highest in NBA history. **Chris Evert** was born in Fort Lauderdale in 1954. During the 1970s and 1980s, she was one of the brightest stars in tennis.

The home of Osceola, James Weldon Johnson, Claude Pepper, and Chris Evert . . .

The number-one state for growing oranges and grapefruit . . .

The site of the nation's oldest town, the John F. Kennedy Space Center, Walt Disney World, and the Everglades . . .

A fascinating land of beaches, shipwrecks, dolphins, and manatees . . .

This is Florida—the Sunshine State!

Did You Know?

There is a town called Christmas not far from Orlando.

If all the oranges Florida grows in a year were laid end to end, they would reach 2 million miles into space. That is like going to the moon and back four times.

Lorenzo Amato made one of the largest pizzas of all time in 1991 near Tallahassee. It was 144 feet in diameter. The pizza was cut into 120,000 slices and was eaten by thirty thousand people.

The original name of the city of Orlando was Jernigan.

The hurricane that struck southern Florida in 1935 produced 200-mile-per-hour winds. During the storm, the barometer fell to 26.35 inches. That was the lowest air pressure ever measured in North or South America.

Chris Evert won the U.S. women's tennis championship in 1975, 1976, 1977, 1978, 1980, and 1982.

One of the world's highest sand castles was made in April 1986 on Treasure Island. It was five stories tall.

President Theodore Roosevelt often came to Florida for deep-sea fishing. Around Captiva Island, he once landed a giant devilfish weighing more than 4,000 pounds.

Florida has a town named Kissimmee. People joke that the name contains the words "kiss me." The name is really a Calusa Indian word, the meaning of which is unknown.

Florida has towns named Jupiter, Venus, and Neptune Beach.

The monster movie *Creature from the Black Lagoon* **was filmed at Wakulla Springs in the 1950s.**

The Miami Dolphins won the Super Bowl football game in 1973 and 1974.

In 1985, Xavier L. Suarez became the first Cuban-born person to be elected mayor of Miami.

One of Florida's first two U.S. senators was David Levy Yulee. He was also the first Jewish U.S. senator. Yulee served in the Senate from 1845 to 1851 and from 1855 to 1861. Florida's Levy County and the town of Yulee were both named for him.

Carrie White, of Palatka, lived to the age of 116. She was the world's oldest known person when she died in 1991.

In 1982, Florida schoolchildren voted to make the Florida panther the state animal.

FLORIDA INFORMATION

Florida state flag

Florida horse conch

Area: 58,664 square miles (twenty-second among the states in size)

Greatest Distance North to South: 447 miles

Greatest Distance East to West: 361 miles

Coastline: 1,350 miles

Borders: Georgia and Alabama to the north; the Atlantic Ocean to the east; the Straits of Florida and the Gulf of Mexico to the south; the Gulf of Mexico and Alabama to the west

Highest Point: Northwestern Florida's Walton County, 345 feet above sea level (the lowest highest point of the fifty states)

Lowest Point: Sea level, along the Atlantic and Gulf coasts

Hottest Recorded Temperature: 109°F. (at Monticello on June 29, 1931)

Coldest Recorded Temperature: -2°F. (at Tallahassee on February 13, 1899)

Statehood: The twenty-seventh state, on March 3, 1845

Origin of Name: Florida is a Spanish word meaning "Full of Flowers." Ponce de León chose that name either because of the wildflowers he saw there or because it was Eastertime, known to the Spaniards as *Pascua Florida*.

Capital: Tallahassee

Counties: 67

United States Representatives: 23 (as of 1992)

State Senators: 40

State Representatives: 120

State Song: "Old Folks at Home," commonly known as "Swanee River," by Stephen Foster

State Motto: In God We Trust

State Nickname: "Sunshine State"

Sabal palm trees

State Seal: Adopted in 1868; revised versions adopted in 1935, 1969, and 1985

State Flag: Adopted in 1899

State Flower: Orange Blossom

State Bird: Mockingbird

State Tree: Sabal palm

State Animal: Florida panther

State Marine Mammal: Manatee

State Saltwater Mammal: Dolphin

State Saltwater Fish: Sailfish

State Freshwater Fish: Largemouth bass

State Shell: Horse conch

State Beverage: Orange juice

State Gem: Moonstone

Florida panther

Some Rivers: Suwannee, St. Johns, St. Marys, Apalachicola

Some Islands: Florida Keys, Ten Thousand Islands, Cedar Keys

Wildlife: Whales, dolphins, manatees, loggerhead sea turtles, alligators, deer, Florida panthers, bears, bobcats, foxes, beavers, otters, skunks, pelicans, storks, mockingbirds, woodpeckers, cranes, herons, bald eagles, egrets, water turkeys

Fishing Products: Shrimp, lobsters, crabs, oysters, sponges, scallops, pompano, red snappers, groupers, mullets

Farm Products: Oranges, grapefruit, sugarcane, lemons, limes, avocados, tomatoes, bananas, strawberries, watermelons, peanuts, peas, celery, cantaloupes, pineapples, beef cattle, milk, chickens

Mining Products: Phosphate rock, oil, limestone

Manufactured Products: Packaged foods, computers, telephones, furniture, paper, fertilizer, cigars, chemicals, robots, missiles, airplanes, spacecraft

Population: 12,937,926, fourth among the states (1990 U.S. Census Bureau figures)

Major Cities (1990 Census):

Jacksonville	635, 230	St. Petersburg	238, 629
Miami	358, 548	Hialeah	188, 004
Tampa	280, 015	Orlando	164, 693
		Fort Lauderdale	149, 377

Mockingbird

FLORIDA HISTORY

Spaniards began to build St. Augustine's Castillo de San Marcos in 1672.

About 10,000 B.C.—Prehistoric Indians live in Florida

A.D. 1513—Ponce de León explores and names Florida, which he claims for Spain

1521—Ponce de León begins a colony in Florida; it fails, and he is killed by Native Americans

1539—Hernando de Soto explores Florida for Spain

1564—The French build Fort Caroline near present-day Jacksonville

1565—Spaniards drive out the French and found St. Augustine

1672—Spaniards begin work on St. Augustine's Castillo de San Marcos, now the oldest stone fort in the United States

1698—Spaniards found Pensacola

1740—English troops from Georgia invade Florida but fail to take it from the Spanish

1763—The English take control of Florida by trading Havana, Cuba, to Spain for the region

1775—The Revolutionary War against England begins

1783—The Americans win the Revolutionary War; as part of the peace treaty, Florida is returned to Spain

1814—During the War of 1812, American general Andrew Jackson captures Pensacola from Spain

1821—Florida becomes part of the United States

1817-18—The Seminoles are defeated by Andrew Jackson in the First Seminole War

1835-42—Osceola and many other Indians are killed during the Second Seminole War; most of the surviving Seminoles are moved to Oklahoma

1845—Florida becomes the twenty-seventh state on March 3

1853—The University of Florida is founded

1861—Florida secedes from the Union and joins the Confederacy; the Civil War begins

1864—The Confederates win the Battle of Olustee on
    February 20

1865—The Confederates save Tallahassee by winning the Battle
    of Natural Bridge; the South loses the war

1868—Florida again becomes part of the United States

1894-95—The "Great Freeze" ruins much of the orange crop

1896—Miami is founded

1900—Florida's population tops half a million

1917-1918—After the United States enters World War I, about
    forty-two thousand Floridians serve

1926-1939—Banks, hotels, and restaurants close as a depression
    hits Florida

1928—A hurricane kills about eighteen hundred people

1935—A hurricane kills more than four hundred people

1938—The Overseas Highway to the Florida Keys opens

1941-1945—More than 250,000 Floridians help the United
    States and its allies win World War II

1950—Florida's population reaches nearly 2.8 million

1958—*Explorer I*, the first U.S. space satellite, is launched from
    Cape Canaveral

1961—The launch of the first American into space is made from
    Cape Canaveral

1969—The first spacecraft to land men on the moon, *Apollo 11*,
    blasts off from Cape Canaveral

1971—Walt Disney World opens near Orlando

1977—The new twenty-two-story state capitol building opens in
    Tallahassee

1980—Miami is torn by race riots

1985—Xavier L. Suarez becomes the first Cuban-born person
    to be elected mayor of Miami

1990—Florida's population reaches nearly 13 million

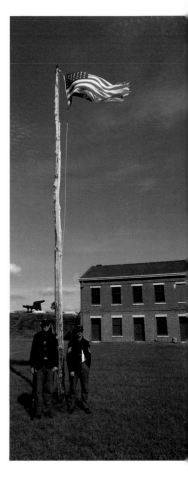

*Fort Clinch, in
Fernandina Beach,
was occupied by Union
troops in 1864.*

59

MAP KEY

Apalachicola River	A,B3	Florida Keys	H7,8	Monticello	A4	Sanibel Island	F6
Apalachicola	B3	Fort Lauderdale	F8	Naples	F6	Sarasota	E6
Atlantic Ocean	A,B,C8	Fort Myers	F6	Neptune Beach	A7	St. Johns River	B7
Cape Canaveral	D8	Gainesville	B6	Orange Park	B6	St. Marys River	A6,7
Captiva Island	F6	Gulf of Mexico	E3,4	Orange City	C7	Straits of Florida	H8
Cedar Keys	C5	Hollywood	F8	Orlando	C7	Suwannee River	B5
Chipley	A3	Jacksonville	A6	Ormond Beach	C7	Tallahassee	A4
Christmas	C7	Jupiter	E8	Palatka	B6,7	Tampa	D6
Clearwater	D5	Key Largo	G8	Pelican Island National		Tampa Bay	D,E5,6
Coral Gables	G8	Key West	H6	Wildlife Refuge	D8	Tarpon Springs	D5
Crescent City	B7	Kissimmee	D7	Pensacola	A1	Ten Thousand Islands	G7
Daytona Beach	C7	Lake Okeechobee	E7,8	Perdido River	A1	Venus	E7
Everglades	G7,8	Manatee River	E6	Port Orange	C7	Vero Beach	D8
Fernandina Beach	A7	Miami	G8	Saint Petersburg	D5	West Palm Beach	F8
Flagler Beach	B7	Miami Beach	F8	Saint Augustine	B7	Yulee	A6,7

GLOSSARY

allies: Nations that help one another, especially during a war

ancient: Relating to those living at a time early in history

billion: A thousand million (1,000,000,000)

capital: The city that is the seat of government

capitol: The building in which the government meets

civil rights: The rights of a citizen

coast: The land along a large body of water

colony: A settlement outside a parent country and ruled by the parent country

composer: The creator of a piece of music

Confederate States of America: The country the South formed at the start of the Civil War; also known as the Confederacy

Congress: The group of people who make the laws for the United States; made up of the Senate and the House of Representatives

coquina: A rock made of shells and coral

drug addicts: People who depend heavily on illegal drugs

everglade: A swampy grassland

Fountain of Youth: A mythical body of water that supposedly could make old people young again

hurricanes: Huge storms that form over oceans

interior: The part of a region away from the coast

key: A low island or reef

kidnap: To take persons away against their will

mammals: Animals that feed their young with mother's milk; human beings, whales, dolphins, and manatees are all mammals

manufacturing: The making of products

mastodons: Large, hairy prehistoric animals that were related to our modern elephants

million: A thousand thousand (1,000,000)

mission: A settlement based around a church; a place where religious work is carried on

oceanarium: A place where ocean animals are kept for public viewing

panhandle: A narrow strip of land connected to a larger piece of land

permanent: Lasting

rebel: To oppose the authority of a government

satellite: A vehicle made to orbit the moon, the earth, or another planet

springs: A place from which water comes out of a crack in the ground

swamp: Wet, marshy land sometimes covered with water

tourism: The business of providing such services as food and lodging for travelers

unions: Groups that fight for the rights of working people

PICTURE ACKNOWLEDGMENTS

Front cover, © Warren Morgan/H. Armstrong Roberts; 1, © Eric Futran Photography; 2, Tom Dunnington; 3, © Brian Parker/Tom Stack & Associates; 4-5, Tom Dunnington; 6-7, © SuperStock; 8 (left), © D. Campione/H. Armstrong Roberts; 8 (map), courtesy of Hammond, Incorporated, Maplewood, New Jersey; 9 (top), © SuperStock; 9 (bottom), © M. Barrett/H. Armstrong Roberts; 10 (top), © Tony Arruza; 10 (bottom left), © Cameramann International, Ltd.; 10 (bottom right), © Steve Elmore/Tony Stone Worldwide/Chicago Ltd.; 11 (left), © SharkSong, M. Kazmers/ Dembinsky Photo Associates; 11 (right), © Larry Lipsky/Tom Stack & Associates; 12, © Stan Osolinski/Dembinsky Photo Associates; 13, © Stan Osolinski/Dembinsky Photo Associates; 14, © Terry A. Renna/Journalism Services; 15, North Wind Picture Archives; 16, North Wind Picture Archives; 18 (top), Florida State Archives, hand coloring North Wind Picture Archives; 18 (bottom), © W. Metzen/H. Armstrong Roberts; 20, Historical Pictures Service, Chicago; 21, North Wind Picture Archives; 22, Florida State Archives; 23, Florida State Archives; 24 (top), Florida State Archives; 24 (bottom), Florida State Archives; 25, Florida State Archives; 26, Florida State Archives; 27, Florida State Archives; 28, © James Quinn/Journalism Services; 29 (both pictures), Florida State Archives; 30, © Eric Futran Photography; 31 (top), © Bill Bachmann/Southern Stock Photos; 31 (bottom), © Cameramann International, Ltd.; 32 (left), © Randy G. Taylor/Southern Stock Photos; 32 (right), © Cameramann International, Ltd.; 33 (left), © Eric Futran Photography; 33 (right), © Tony Arruza; 34-35, © SuperStock; 36, © Virginia R. Grimes; 37 (left), © W. Bertsch/H. Armstrong Roberts; 37 (right), © Camerique Stock Photography/H. Armstrong Roberts; 38, © Gregory Murphey/Journalism Services; 39 (top), © Joan Dunlop; 39 (bottom), © SuperStock; 40 (top), © Doug Armand/Tony Stone Worldwide/Chicago Ltd.; 40 (bottom), © Mark E. Gibson/Marilyn Gartman Agency; 41, © James Blank/Root Resources; 42, AP/Wide World Photos; 43 (left), © Gail Nachel/Root Resources; 43 (right), © W. Bertsch/H. Armstrong Roberts; 44 (top), Florida Dept. of Commerce, Div. of Tourism; 44 (bottom), © Photri; 45, © W. Metzen/H. Armstrong Roberts; 46, © Mark E. Gibson/Marilyn Gartman Agency; 47 (left), © Richard L. Capps/R/C Photo Agency; 47 (right), © Brian Parker/Tom Stack & Associates; 48, Florida State Archives; 50 (both pictures), AP/Wide World Photos; 51, Wide World Photos, Inc.; 52 (both pictures), Wide World Photos, Inc.; 53 (both pictures), AP/Wide World Photos; 54 (bottom), © M. Thonig/H. Armstrong Roberts; 54-55 (top), Florida Dept. of Commerce, Div. of Tourism; 55 (bottom), Bob Self/*Florida Times-Union;* 56 (top), courtesy Flag Research Center, Winchester, Massachusetts 01890; 56 (bottom), Florida Dept. of Commerce, Div. of Tourism; 57 (top), © Steve Elmore/Tony Stone Worldwide/Chicago Ltd.; 57 (middle), © SharkSong, M. Kazmers/Dembinsky Photo Associates; 57 (bottom), © Stan Osolinski/Dembinsky Photo Associates; 58, © SuperStock; 59, © W. Metzen/H. Armstrong Roberts; 60, Tom Dunnington; back cover, © Tom Algire Photography/SuperStock

INDEX

Page numbers in boldface type indicate illustrations.

Adderley, Julian "Cannonball," 52
Amato, Lorenzo, 54
animals, 5, 11-13, **11**, **12**, **13**, 15, 38, 39, 40, **40**, 44, 45, 46, **46**, 47, **47**, 55, **56**, 57, **57**
Apalachicola River, 9, 19
Asians, 31
Atlantic Ocean, 8, 39, 42
Atocha (ship), 42 **42**
"Baby Corps," 23
Bartow, **24**
baseball, 43, 52, **53**
basketball, 41, 52-53
beaches, 36, **36**, 38-39
Bethune, Mary McLeod, 39
Bethune-Cookman College, 39
birds, 12, 13, **13**, 39, 40, **40**, 57, **57**
Biscayne Bay, 24-25
black people (African Americans), 4, 22-23, 28-29, **29**, 31, 39, 50-51
Blue Angels, **44**, 45
bordering states, 8, 56
Busch Gardens, 44, **44**
Butterfly World, 39
Cape Canaveral, **14**, 27, 39
Captiva Island, 43, 54
Caribbean islands, 16-17
Carlson, Steve, 52
Castillo de San Marcos, 37-38, **37**, **58**
Christmas (town), 54
civil rights, 28-29, 50-51
Civil War, 22-23, **23**, **59**
Clearwater, 43
climate, 13, 24, 36, 54, 56
Coastal Plains region, 9
coconuts, **10**
Columbus, Christopher, 16-17
Confederate States of America, 22-23
Coral Gables, 25
coral reefs, 42
Creature from the Black Lagoon, 55
Crystal River, **9**
Cuba and Cubans, 16, 28, **29**, 40, 55
Cypress Gardens, **9**

Daytona Beach, 38-39, **39**
Daytona International Speedway, 38-39, **39**
Destin, **8**
Douglas, Marjory Stoneman, 52, **52**
drug problems, 29
education, 29, 39, 46
English rule, 19-20
EPCOT Center, **28**, 36, 46
Everglades, 9, **13**, 47, **47**, 52, **Back Cover**
Evert, Chris, 4, 53, **53**, 54
explorers, Spanish, 16-18, 42
Fairchild Tropical Garden, **10**
farming, 4, 16, 22, **22**, 24, 32, 45, 57
Fernandina Beach, 38, **59**
fish, 11, **11**, **30**, 54, 57
Fisher, Mel, 42, **42**
fishing, 33, 54, 57
flag of Florida, **56**, 57
Flagler, Henry Morrison, 24-25, **25**, 50
Florida Keys, **3**, 6-7, 10, 12, 41-42, **41**
Florida Uplands region, 9-10
flowers, 10, **10**
football, 5, 37, 40-41, 44, 55
Fort Caroline, 18, **18**, 36
Fort Clinch, **59**
Fort King, **21**
Fort Lauderdale, 25, 39
Fort Myers, 43
Foster, Stephen, 9, 56
Gainesville, 46
Gator Bowl, 37
geography of Florida, 8, 56, 57
Gilmore, Artis, 52-53
gold, 17, 42, **42**
Gooden, Dwight, 52, **53**
Gorrie, John, 49
government jobs, 33
government of Florida, 22, 45, **45**, 56

grapefruit, 4, 24, 32, 45
Great Depression, 26
Gulf of Mexico coast, 8, 42-45
Haiti, 28
Hawaii, 8
Hemingway, Ernest, 5, 42
Hialeah, 25
Hispanic people, 28, **29**, 31, 40, 55
history of Florida, 4, 15-29, 36, 37-38, 39, 42, 44, 45, 49, 54, 55, 58-59
Hollywood, 25
hurricanes, 13, 17, 25, 42, 54
Indians (Native Americans), 4, 15-16, **15**, **16**, 17, 18, 20-22, **21**, 31, 45, **48**, 49, 54
industry, 31-33, 36, 40, 57
islands, 10, **36**, 41-42, **41**, 43, **43**, 57
Jackson, Andrew, 20-21, **20**
Jacksonville, 18, 36-37
jobs, 29, 31-33
John F. Kennedy Space Center, 4, 39, **39**
John Pennekamp Coral Reef State Park, 42
Johnson, James Weldon, 4, 50
Jupiter (town), 55
Key Biscayne, **6-7**
Key Largo, 42
Key West, 42
Kingsley Plantation, 36
Kissimmee, 54
Lake Okeechobee, 9, 25
lakes, 9
Lincoln, Abraham, 22
Louisiana, 19
manatees, 11, **11**, 46
manufacturing, 31-32, **32**, 40, 57
maps of Florida showing:
    cities and geographical features, **60**
    location in U.S. **2**
    products and history, **4-5**
    topography, **8**

Marco Island, **36**
Marineland of Florida, 38
Menéndez de Avilés, Pedro, 18
Miami, 24-25, 28, 40-41, **40**, 55
Miami Beach, 25, **26**, 40, **Front Cover**
Miami Dolphins, 5, 55
Miami Heat, 41
mining, 57
Mississippi, 19
Monkey Jungle, 40
museums, 37, 38, 43, **43**, 45
name, origin of, 10, 17, 56
Naples, 43
Natural Bridge, Battle of, 23
Neptune Beach, 55
nickname, Florida's , 4, 56
Oklahoma, 21
Olustee, Battle of, 23
Orange Bowl, 40-41
oranges, **1**, 4, 24, 32, 45, 54, **54**
Orlando, 28, 46, **46**, 54
Ormond Beach, 38
Osceola, 4, 21, **21**, **48**, 49
Overseas Highway, 41-42, **41**
Palatka, 55
panther, Florida, 12-13, 47, 55, **57**
Parrot Jungle, **10**, 40, **40**
Pelican Island National Wildlife Refuge, 39
Pensacola, 17, **20**, **23**, 45, **45**
Pensacola Naval Air Station, 45, **45**
people of Florida, 27-28, **28**, **30**, 31, **31**, 40
Pepper, Claude, 51, **51**
Perdido River, 9
pirates, 44
pizza, huge, 54
Plant, Henry, 24
plants, 10-11, **57**

Poitier, Sidney, 52, **52**
pollution, 29
Ponce de León, Juan, 17
population, 27-28, 29, 31, 33, 36, 40, 57
prehistoric Florida, 15-16, 45
products of Florida, **1**, 4, **4-5**, 24, **30**, 31-33, **32**, **33**, 36, 40, 54, **54**, 57
Puerto Rico, 17
railroads, 24-25, **24**
Randolph, A. Philip, 50-51, **50**
Rawlings, Marjorie Kinnan, 5, **51**, 51
Revolutionary War , 19-20
Ringling Brothers and Barnum and Bailey Circus, 43
rivers, 9, **9**, 11, 36, 57
Roosevelt, Theodore, 39, 54
St. Augustine, 4, 17, 18, **18**, 37-38, **37**, **58**
St. Johns River, 9, 36
St. Marys River, 9
St. Petersburg, 43-44
Salt River, **9**
sand castle, huge, 54, **54-55**
Sanibel Island, 43, **43**
Sarasota, 43, **43**
schools, 29, 39, 46, 55
scuba diving, **3**
Sea World, 46, **46**
Seminole wars, 20-22, **20**, **21**, 49
senior citizens, 28, 31, 51
settlers, 17-18, 20, 22, 23-24, 45
shells and shellfish, 11, 16, 33, **33**, 43, **43**, **56**, 57
size of Florida, 56
slavery, 22-23, **22**, 36
South, **2**, 8, 22-23
space program, 4, **14**, 27, 36, 39, **39**
Spanish explorers, 16-18, 42
Spanish rule, 18, 20-21

sports, **3**, 4, 5, 37, 40-41, 43, 44, 52-53, **53**, 54, 55
springs, 45-46
state capitol, 5, 45, **45**
state symbols, 12, 55, **56**, 57, **57**
statehood, 22, 56
Straits of Florida, 8
Stranahan, Ivy Cromartie, 39
Suarez, Xavier L., 55
"Sunshine State," 4
Super Bowl, 55
Suwannee River, 9
swamps, 9, 12, **12**, 21, 23, 47, **47**
"Swanee River" (song), 9, 56
Tallahassee, 22, 23, **27**, **29**, 45, **45**
Tampa, 24, 44, **44**
Tampa Bay, 43, 44
Tampa Bay Buccaneers, 5, 44
Tarpon Springs, 33
Ten Thousand Islands, 10
tennis, 4, 53, **53**, 54
topography of Florida, **8**, 9-10, 56
tourism, 25, 26, 28, 31, **32**, 40
Treasure Island, 54, **54-55**
treasures, sunken, 42, **42**, 45
trees, 9, 10-11, **10**, 45, 57
Tuttle, Julia S., 24, **24**
University of Florida, 46
Venus (town), 55
Vero Beach, 38
Virginia colony, 19
Wakulla Springs, 46, 55
Walt Disney World, 4, 28, **28**, **34-35**, 36, 46
West Indies, 17
West Palm Beach, 38, **38**
White, Carrie, 55, **55**
World War I, 25
World War II, 25, **25**, **26**
Yulee, David Levy, 55

ABOUT THE AUTHOR

Dennis Brindell Fradin is the author of more than one hundred published children's books. His works for Childrens Press include the Young People's Stories of Our States series, the Diaster! series, and the Thirteen Colonies series. His other books are *Remarkable Children* (Little, Brown) and *How I Saved the World* (Dillon). Dennis is married to Judith Bloom Fradin, a high-school English teacher. They have two sons, Tony and Mike, and a daughter, Diana. Dennis graduated from Northwestern University in 1967 with a B.A. in creative writing, and has lived in Evanston, Illinois, since that year.